Acclaim for DINO FOXX

WHEN THE GLITTER FADES

In this collection, Dino Foxx utilizes those elements of life that make us most vulnerable – truth, pain, loss, family, fear, love, uncertainty, and healing – and he weaves stories into poems into stories into poems, over and over, again and again. And although they depict the experiences of one man, these poems are the corridos of our jotito youth and of San Anto's raza. Through them, Dino Foxx masterfully demonstrates that he is one true, firm-footed, literary badass.

> **Jesús Alonzo**, author of *Jotos del Barrio*
> and *Miss America: A Mexicanito Fairy's Tale*

For over a hundred and fifty years in the heart of South Texas, a bloated, public works project dedicated to shoring up white, straight privileges has toiled ceaselessly, day and night, through weekends and holidays. For the queers, Latino/as, and the doubly blessed queer Latino/as who live here, the task of inventing the self, claiming a space, holding onto family, celebrating life and negotiating relationships with Mexico, Tejas, Mexicanidad and the greater Latinidad remain bold ambitions, if not key challenges. *When the Glitter Fades* is Dino Foxx's multi-layered snapshot of that struggle taking place in San Antonio at the dawn of a new century. It is a compelling glimpse into one young man's *corazón sagrado* beating out a zealous love for humanity to disco, cumbia, and conjunto.

> **Dr. Paul Bonin-Rodriguez**
> Performance as Public Practice, University of Texas, Austin

Filled with insurgent testimony, this work stands as a cathartic monument dedicated to a life lived and living large. All at once vulnerable, revealing and unrelenting in its brutal candor, each poem is like a postcard declaring, "I was here!" stepping stones continuing the journey onward and upward. These are love poems...as dynamic and tumultuous as the relationships they capture. In true Aristotelian tradition, the poetic drama catapults these ordinary experiences of everyday life to the level of heroic standards. There is sharp wit here and brassy humor in poems that strut the fine line of being both highly readable and performative. Smooth from page to stage. Dino's work reminds me of *how* brave it is to love and to surrender to it. I caught myself snapping my fingers, shaking my head to the familiar, and bursting out in laughter as he manages to say everything we've all known about loving all along, but didn't know how to describe. Our first love and last love is self-love. He gets it, he gets to it, and serves it up raw and un-cut to the rest of us! Now go get some! Delicious.

> **Angela Kariotis**, Playwright

WHEN THE GLITTER FADES

WHEN THE GLITTER FADES

POEMS BY **DINO FOXX**

FOREWORD BY RITA URQUIJO-RUIZ, PHD

Kórima Press

Credits:
"Exotic" appeared in *Queer Codex: Chile Love* (*allgo*/Evelyn Street Press, 2004).

"Dia de los Muertos" appeared in *Suspect Thoughts: A Journal of Subversive Writting*, Issue # 19, 2007.

"Thin Line" and "Broken Spanish" appeared in *Mariposas: A Modern Anthology of Queer Latino Poetry* (Floricanto Press, 2008)

"You Never Change," "All In the Family," "Hollow," and "Withdrawal" appeared in *Tragic Bitches: An Experiment in Queer Xicana & Xicano Performance Poetry* (Kórima Press).

Cover Concept: Dino Foxx, Logan Magz
Cover Photographer: Troy Wise [www.troywisephotography.com]
Book Design: Lorenzo Herrera y Lozano

Published by Kórima Press
San Francisco, CA
www.korimapress.com

ISBN: 978-0-9889673-2-8

For Lorenzo Herrera y Lozano, for loving me through the poetry, bad haircuts, late-night snacks, missed flights, road trips, bad hotel rooms, and heartbreaks. Thank you for filling my life with laughter and adventure.

CONTENTS

FOREWORD
by Rita Urquijo-Ruiz, Ph.D.

GLITTERY POETICS:
JOTEANDO EN SAN ANTONIO, TEJAS

> I struggle to "talk" from the wound's gash, make
> sense of the deaths and destruction, and pull the
> pieces of my life back together. I yearn to pass on
> to the next generation the spiritual activism I've
> inherited from my cultures.
>
> –Gloria E. Anzaldúa
> "Let us be the healing of the wound"

The poetry of Dino Foxx is not for the saintly (gente persignada) or faint of heart. Still, anyone who is courageous enough to read it, or better yet, witness it when he performs it, will feel the transformation while, at his invitation, entering into the poet's home, barrio, body, heart, and soul. As the master of these geographic and cultural spaces, Dino will guide us through the painful, but also through the sweet, parts of these terrains. He will challenge and encourage us while sharing his most intimate regions as we witness every blow, every beso, every punch, every deseo, every cut, every sonrisa, every insult, every abrazo, every bite, every cuento.

As witnesses, we must trust but also participate in Dino's rituals; beholding is not enough. Not with the artist sharing so much of himself that touches us profundamente while "reflecting" our own struggles. He survives hunger (in body and soul), abuse (of many types), and des-amor (from family and lovers) in order to create and nurture a proud, irrepressible, loving, xicano-tejano-joto artista and activista. Dino is a true "artivista," as Martha Gonzalez and others, call all artists who practice activism and inspire their communities through/with their art and vision.

But where is home for this poet? What place(s) could possibly influence his creation? Given the geographic location of Texas, the proximity of this enormous state to Mexico as well as to the U.S. south, it is no coincidence that it is here, more precisely in San Antonio's West Side, where Dino was born and became the sparkling, shimmering, glittery Joto of now. But the glitter didn't always stick. It took him many years and tears to ready himself for the world. His poetry, as well as his performance work, shines in the true fashion of (t)his community that appropriately encourages its members to go forth and do well by shouting "Dale Shine!!" And Dino fiercely does!

The brilliance of this collection exists in the Joto-Poeta being a sinvergüenza shamelessly exposing himself and his familial environment in order to heal and to create a new reality, a new family that will accept and love the Xicano Joto in all his splendor. Therefore, Dino introduces us to his mama's life, hands, comforting food, teachings, vanity, wit y ganas inmensas to survive; to his tías' laughter and chisme at his grandma's kitchen table; to his first sexual, playful, s/m encounter with his little primo; to his desire for male bodies that remind him of his tíos; to his absent, abusive, biological father but also his hard-working, undocumented, monolingual Spanish-speaking, responsible, loving Daddy who adopted his family; to good and bad lovers; to great and painful fucking; to sweet and bitter experiences; to fun and harsh nights out; to linguistic maromas and grammatically incorrect love-making, to fitting in and feeling alienated.

The book is divided into five sections entitled *High-Kicks & Handcuffs, Untitled Childhood, Broken Spanish, Fool's Paradise,* and *Chasing Scars Away.*

The title poem of the first section places us at a huge queer bar with overpriced, weak drinks by cute bartenders, where divas that have the privilege can skip to the front of the line; these are memories of drunken, fun nights seducing men, as the poet attempts to dance in chanclas like a back up dancer and falling on his ass; and later on, the arrest where the "SAPD squad car 7334 drove away / With [his] heart and [his] life in the backseat." In the same section, the poem "Not Xicano Enough," criticizes the community's exigencies of cultural and ethnic identity by presenting a litany of details about a traditional, heteronormative Chicana/o life in San Antonio, as the author hopes to incorporate his childhood memories into the national imaginary. "Exotic" highlights a relationship with a closeted "heteroflexible" man and the poet refusing to teach him about being openly queer: "I don't wanna be your exotic, homoerotic, / Man-whore, boy toy fantasy."

In "Untitled Childhood," the poem that also titles the second section, we see two boys, cousins, kissing each other but also pretending to fight like their parents, exhibiting the violence they have learned from their families. "All in the Family" highlights an irrepressible aunt who serves as a role model to the poet by being single and independent. "Daddy" pays homage to a hard-working, undocumented, loving man who adopts the poet's broken family. Section three contains "Sleep Sounds" a poem with the sweetest of images:

Now, bedtime is when I explore
Your beautiful body, kneading
The stress away with love. It is the series
Of besitos that I leave across your back
And the goose bumps rising on your flesh

In the title poem in section four, "Fool's Paradise," there's an attempt to ignore the failure of a broken relationship by still sleeping and loving each other foolishly even after being broken up more than a year. But this section also contains "A Fucking Poem" that simply states:

I want you to fuck a good poem out of me.
Not a poem about animalistic, lust but
Candles lit, soft music playing kind of lovemaking.
The kind I have never been comfortable enough
To experience while sober.

I want you to lick the insecurity off of my skin.
Insecurity from years of being told fat is ugly
And from guys who treated my body like
Something that wasn't worth worshiping.

The whole collection closes with "Dos Poetas Locos," about the type of man who inspires poetry for the author:

I was saving this poem for you.
I hid it in my entire being and lived it
Before I could capture it on paper to
Give to you as a gift of thanks. A thank
You for the uncontrollable laughter,
The tears, the history, the food, the
Drink, the movement, the sweat, and the
Arte that we let our souls create
In a time where many find it hard
To catch a single glimpse of light.

I was saving this poem for you.
Now, it is yours forever.

This poem is the perfect ending to this book given that as readers, we also become owners of Dino Foxx's experiences and poetry by the time we arrive at the culmination of this, his most loving and powerful gift. May those who have the audacity to accompany him throughout his journey, share their privilege with others who will receive an opportunity and a fearless camino of survival and triumph.

Rita E. Urquijo-Ruiz, Ph.D.
San Antonio, TX
May 24, 2013

ACKNOWLEDGMENTS

This project would have not been possible if it weren't for an entire village of beautiful, supportive and loving people. To everyone who served as a support system, sounding board, source of inspiration and friend throughout this process, my eternal gratitude.

To my loving mama who taught me how to tell stories, how to laugh with every ounce of my being, and how to love and be loved in return. These hands are not more like, and I promise to tell your story to help change the world. To my supportive daddy and loving brother, your silent strong ways keep me grounded. To the tías for teaching me comedic timing and that you never really stop growing. And to my primas for the countless hours of mischief and laughter.

This work was created with generous support from two very important communities. To my allgo familia: Ana Sisnett, Jesús Ortega, Orlando Ramírez, Martha Ramos-Duffer, Sheree Ross, Miramar Dichoso, Jax Cuevas, Jen Margulies, Clemencia Zapata, Rose Pulliam, Candace López, Melissa Galvan, J.J. Lara, Wendy Joy Martínez, and of course Priscilla A. Hale and Lorenzo Herrera y Lozano for taking me in, giving me unconditional love and giving me the resources to capture these stories.

To my Jump-Start Performance Co. family: Sterling Houston, Paul Bonin-Rodriguez, Monessa Esquivel, Chayo Zaldivar, Paul Harford, Kim Corbin, Chuck Squire, Robert Rehm, Kitty Williams, Sheila Sisler-Currie, Craig Pennel, Annele Spector, Lisa Suárez, Erik Bosse, Felice García, María Salazar, Nita Langer, Dolly Miller, Oscar Alvarado, Olupero Aiyenimelo, Victoria García, Pamela Dean Kenny, Michele Brinkley and C.C. Brinkley. For teaching me how to be fearless, glamorous, fierce and for giving me the gift of fire.

To the creative team that first brought these words to the stage when this project still had another name: S.T. Shimi, Billy Muñoz, Daniel Jackson, Sandy Dunn, David Currie and Amanda Ireta. For their love, their talent, their creativity, their patience and trust. It finally happened!

To my herman@s in pen: Emanuel Xavier, Anel I. Flores, Jesús Alonzo, Joe Jiménez, María Limón, Elaine Mica Pérez, Laurie Dietrich, Charles Rice-Gonzalez, Manuel Cros Esquivel, Pablo Miguel Martínez, Rita Urquijo-Ruiz, Adele Adkins, kt shorb, Ana-Maurine Lara, Sara Beth Bareilles, Natalie Goodnow, Wura-Natasha Ogunji, Adelina Anthony, Marvin K. White, Mike Sinfuegos, Vincent Toro, Grisel Acosta, Laurie Ann Guerrero, Hector Bojórquez and Virginia Grise. Thank you for being a constant source of inspiration and for being the most badass network of writers that a jotito could have!

To my burly-Q family for helping me find the glitter and for teaching me that (even when you want it to) the glitter is never really gone. Miss Black Orchid, Blue Valentine, Suki Jones, Miss Lucky Strike, Pystol Whips, Squirrely Temple, Candy Kane, Gooughie Gomez, Goldie Candela, Chola Magnolia, Jasper St. James, Gaige, Vixy Van Hellen, Pelvis Costello, The Stripping Granny, Stephan Gaeth, Eaton Johnson, Shelby Mines, Cruel Valentine, Camille T. Oe, Remi Martini, Sin O'Rita, Benni Atchison and Coco Lectric.

To the maestr@s who I have had the honor and privilege to work with and learn from. To Steve Bailey, Guillermo Gómez-Peña, Sharon Bridgforth, Robert Karimi, Teo Castellanos, Viera Dubacova, Jaro Vinarsky, Diane Malone, Sterling Houston and Raquel Araujo Madera for helping me sharpen my pencil and fine-tune my machine.

To the women who are responsible for enabling my addiction to the stage, please take your bow. Alicia Fernandez, Liv Downen, Kimberly Contreras,

Janie Sauceda, Crystol Don, Julie Balderrama, Cassandra Parker-Nowicki, Rachel Rangel, Brandi Fortelny and Patricia Nolan Moy.

The development of this work could not have been possible without the generous support of: City of Austin through the Economic Growth & Redevelopment Services Office/Cultural Arts Division, San Antonio Dance Umbrella, The Electric Performance Lab, Department for Culture and Creative Development (City of San Antonio), Alternate Roots, Kronkosky Charitable Foundation, the Texas Commission on the Arts, theFund, Raúl R. Salinas, René Valdez, David Zamora-Casas, Dr. Arturo Baca, Leonardo Toro, Irene Mata, Genevieve Rodriguez, Mario Cortes, Marissa Vásquez, Victor Richardson, J.A. Trujillo, Robert Sturm, Melissa Hidalgo, Sarah Guerra, Michaela Díaz-Sánchez, Pepe Aguilar-Hernández, Michael Hames-García and Eric-Christopher García .

To my loving partner, Logan Magz, for his patience and understanding, thank you for showing me how to laugh, and dance and for inspiring me to be a more dedicated, organized, well-groomed and fearless artist. I love you, Monkey.

Lastly, to the men who were captured in this book during the 13 years it took to create it…you will never be forgotten.

WHEN THE
GLITTER
FADES

I. HIGH-KICKS & HANDCUFFS

NOT XICANO ENOUGH

Maybe it's just me,
But I've always felt the need
To prove myself to the world.
Beyond the superficial,
Not being skinny enough,
not hot enough
And not butch enough.
When I began to explore my heritage
I found out that
I'm not Mexican enough!

I started going to Cesar Chavez
Marches and wearing my *"Uvas No!"*
Button, but every time I'd show up
To any Xicano reading or gallery
Showing, I would not find acceptance
Among these people who looked like me
Because I lived on the north side.

I shouldn't feel bad about that.
I grew up on the west side.
But I don't get my Xicano privileges back.
Want me to prove that I'm down?
Then let's play.
I won't trip and say I know the pain of
Working long hours in the sun
Picking grapes or strawberries.
I don't know what it's like to swim across
The Rio Grande to start a new life.
I've never worked in factories
Under poor conditions.

But I work for, fight for, and hurt
For, all those who do.
Because they are my gente.

I come from a long line of proud,
Well-educated Chicano people.
Mnah! ¡Pos órale!
Dale chine, holmes!
I can hang with the best.
Grew up with the smell of fresh tortillas
On the comal every Sunday morning.
My tía Nancy always handed me a hot one.
I would spread butter on it,
Roll it up, and eat it in three bites.
I know what that's like.
I have searched the damn refrigerator
For five minutes looking for the butter
In countless butter tubs
Only to find beans and left over
Picadillo con papas from two weeks ago.

I'm sorry that my name isn't
Pepe, Chale, Vale, Monolo or Juan…
But those are my uncles.
They are the ones eating breakfast
Every morning at Doña Maria's
Before going to work
In the welding or car shops,
Or the construction site at 36th and Commerce.
Hardworking and hardheaded,
All of them suffering from PMS…
You know, *Pinche Macho Syndrome.*

The same viejos standing along
The back wall at Lizette's debut.
Standing beer in hand
And a foot against the wall.

The same guys dancing
At Flea World with their chicks.
Tight jeans tucked into their botas,
A loud colorful western shirt, and a
Belt buckle the size of a Cutlass Supreme.
Oh, and you better believe that they drive one too!
Like my mom's old one, but different colors.
They have a sarape on the dashboard,
Little bolitas hanging along the top of the
Windshield and a CD hanging
From the rear view mirror.
They have a statue of the Virgen de Guadalupe
Glued to the dash and a huge sticker
On the back window, above the bumper sticker
With the white rose and the words: *Selena Forever*,
Reads the longest last name in the world…
Castilleja-De Los Santos!

I grew up being hit by the chancla,
Filling my panza with Hot Cheetos and Big Red.
I only eat sour pickles if they have a
Chinese candy in the middle of them.
I lived right next door to La Sad Gurl
Strutting down the street squeezed
Into her latest ensemble from Melrose.
Or 5-7-9, even though she knew damn well
She was a size 12.

The plastic straps of her Payless platform shoes
Would hold on for dear life
As she hoofed it to the bus stop
To catch the 82 to the Rivercenter Mall.
She had to meet La Flaca, El Spooky,
El Dreamer and baby Taz for their latest
Image Shot with the red background and
The Chinese Letters.

I went through most of Middle school
With a red spot on the palm
Of my hand from eating Kool-Aid out of it.
It was blood red— my stigmata from
My crucifixion.
But this blood is the same blood
That runs through all their veins.

I gotta be proud of who I am.
I can make fun of what I am.
And this is who I am.
And that's all that I'll ever want to be.
Mnah!

HIGH-KICKS & HANDCUFFS

Pa' Lorenzo Herrera y Lozano

You can keep your overpriced fancy
Aloha register and your broken tip jars.
We're keeping the memories of
Endless nights we spent dancing to the
Beat pouring through speakers
Under a blanket of flashing lights and
Spinning mirrors.

You can keep your bartenders
Way too cute to be mad at for not
Knowing how to pour a strong drink.
We'll keep the money we would
Have spent on bottomless Absolute
Citron Cape Cods and, trust, bitch,
That's a lot of money.

You can keep my VIP Gold Card.
We'll keep the memory of being
Complete rock star divas skipping
Ahead of the line that wrapped around
The block and the looks on
Bitter constipated queens' faces as we
Are rushed on to be let
In without paying cover.

You can keep your Video Bar
Playing all our guilty pleasures.
You can't take away the rhythm
In our hips that seduced countless
Men on that silver dance floor.

You can't take away the night
I ended up on my back, staring at
The ceiling after trying to dance
Like a Britney Spears back-up
Dancer— in chanclas.

You can keep your main dance
Floor with all your shirtless
White boys jumping around
To rhythmless music. We'll
Keep the times we laughed at
The entire room for jumping up
And down to the chorus
Of Kelly Clarkson's
"Since You've Been Gone" and
The más hot attitude we would
Throw, learning to hold
Complete conversations while
Not breathing and keeping our
Stomachs sucked in. Purple
Is our color anyway, gurl.

You can keep your third floor
Grand ballroom and your bad
Lighting. We'll keep the fun we
Had in the hidden restroom and
The funky fresh way we impressed
The whole party with the way we
Leaned with it, and rocked with it,
And popped and locked from left
To right and snapped our fingers,
And how we leaned back. Word.

You can keep your photo booth
Mostly used for minors to
Sneak drinks to enhance their
BX experience. We'll keep
The countless photos we have of
Us in drag on Halloween or of us
Doing dirty things with our
Rosaries. We'll keep the memories
We have of the many boys we kissed
In random places around the club.

You can keep your flying chanclas
And angry ex-boyfriends trying to fight.
We'll keep the countless after-hours
In horrible lighting at house parties or
Las Salsas or Mi Tierra or Mr. Taco;
With menudo or fideo con Carne, Big Red,
Drag queens and carne guisada con cheese.

When SAPD squad car 7334 drove away
With my heart and my life in the backseat
You tried to rob us of 8 years of history.
We find ourselves trying to shake
You like a bad dream, but these memories
Remain there like stretch marks— sad
Little reminders of decadent nights of
The past.

We're forced back down on the Strip
Going to bars that smell like arroz con culo
Or bars that only play good music when
Trying to make a quick buck

Off our people by bringing in a random
Pop en Español artist. There's a huge
Hole in our hearts because of this. But
We'll wait until the memories of the
High-kick seen around the world fade
Or we're too famous for you to care.
We'll once again return to church
For the kind of prayers that can only
Be heard above the loud music of
The Bonham Xchange.

EXOTIC

For Suheir Hammad

I fell in love with a boy.
I fell in love once and I lost completely.

See, he was in love with a girl.
I fell in love with a straight boy.
A heterosexual, better called "heteroflexible."
The only difference between this guy and a gay guy
Is a six-pack of Shiner Bock.

The view from inside the closet must be getting old.
I'm surprised the walls haven't started to close in on you yet.
Kindly be a dear and hand me my coat, it's time for me to go out.
I keep wishing you would follow my lead and leave that dark,
Damp place to see the light of the world and what it could be
For you and me…but it won't happen, and I can't make it happen.
I don't wanna be your exotic, homoerotic,
Man-whore, boy toy fantasy.

I can't be seduced by your half-bred,
Frat boy, truck-driving, faded-t-shirt-wearing,
Low-rise-Levi-jeans-sportin', straight-porn-watching charm.

Don't let yourself be seduced by my difference.
Don't build your fucked up fetish fantasy around
The sway of my hips as I walk away from you.
My milkshake does bring all the boys to the yard, but come on!?
I don't wanna be your exotic, homoerotic,
Man-whore, boy toy fantasy.

I can no longer sit around for you to feel on again.
Won't sit here with my thumb up my ass while you feel off again.

Don't expect me to come running to the phone
When you decide to call, and don't expect me to
Shove my tongue down your throat
When you've finally had enough to drink.

I don't wanna be your exotic, homoerotic,
Man-whore, boy toy fantasy.
I'm sick of your Almond Joy,
"Sometimes ya feel like a nut,
Sometimes ya don't" bullshit mentality.
There are lots of tricks out there who
Would be more than willing to let you use them.
Why did you choose me?

The rhythm with which I move as I stroll
Ain't some spicy, delicious, Latin beat,
It's just a walk, get over it.

I don't wanna be your exotic,
homoerotic, man-whore, boy toy fantasy.
Don't wanna be your Mr. Slave, slut bag,
skank weed, chew toy, circle jerk, j/o buddy,
Reach-around machine, cum hole, fuck hole,
Little piece of the Latin Invasion.
Cuz odds are if I made you step outside
Your little hiding spot, I would have to raise you
Like some sort of gay mother.
Teaching you things learned when you
Finally come out and stop pretending.

It would be as if you were born again and
I don't have time to teach someone how
To live their life when I don't exactly know
How to live my own.
I don't wanna be your first.
Don't wanna be your breath of fresh air,
Your taste of the new world.
I deserve someone who doesn't
Turn me on and off like a light switch.
Don't want to be your exotic.

PUNK FAGGOT BITCH

Flashbacks and pistols in your
Face make wounds
Burst open. Letting fresh
Blood meet cold air.
Once again I have to
Scramble to find a way
To stitch this shit up.
Trying hard not to bleed
All over the carpet.

Suspect No. 1, as
They called him, looked like
Any man I would try to take
Home at the end of a night
Of drinking.
Suspect No. 2, looked
Like my little brother.

They can have my wallet with
Everything in it.
They can take the cash, all
Forms of ID, my $10 Starbucks
Gift card, my TABC
License, my American
Red Cross CPR/First Aid
Card, and my old bank
Receipts showing
How little hard
Working people make.

My size was supposed
To intimidate them.
They weren't afraid
Of some punk faggot bitch.
How did they know? What
Tipped it off? The way I was
Dressed? Would those be the
Words screamed at
Any man to belittle him
Into being afraid?
Or did these words sting too
Much because they rang true?
Those words bite, and scratch
When there are
Two guns being pointed
At you while they are
Screamed in your face.

It's been three days.
I still can't sleep.
I see them there. I hear
Them scream. I see the
Dark bandanas across
Their faces. I feel one
Of them behind me so I
Can't run. I hear
Him demand my money
I hear those words,
Loud and sharp.

Punk...
Faggot...
Bitch...
Punk...
Faggot...
Bitch...

I hear my scream.
I see what I only assume was a weapon
In the pocket of their jackets.
Knowing now it was probably
Just their hands. But in that
Moment, I see myself
Surrendering to them, the way
Oprah said you should when
You find yourself at the
Wrong place at the wrong
Time. I see my wallet in their
Hand, I see them throw my
Car keys. I can see them,
Like mice, scattering over
The grassy hill. I feel
My pulse race as I jump
Behind the wheel of my car.

I hear tires screeching,
smelling of burnt rubber.
I take off without
Shutting my door.
I still hear the cold voice of
The 911 operator. I hear

The frustration in his voice
Build as I try to form
Proper sentences. I hear
Him sternly tell me to pull
Over as I attempt to chase
The getaway car. I feel
My heart pound for the 25
Minutes it took police to
Respond. I hear the
Officer's generic standard
Questions. I can hear
Myself stutter trying to answer.
I remember being distracted
By how gorgeous the police
Officer was. Then he too
Looks at me, and says,
"Wow, I can't believe they
Would mess with you. You're
A big guy." He keeps
Writing on his little notepad.

But there was something
I left out of the police
Report, because I couldn't
Bring myself to tell him.
The words, they screamed,
They didn't just yell: "Give
Me everything you took
Out of the ATM!" They
Screamed more than that.

Words that brought this man
Of large build to his knees.
Words I have heard before,
Yelled exactly the same way.
I hear the words.
Loud and sharp as he
Punched my stomach.
Sharp pain in my rectum
As he shoved himself inside.
That first time,
When I wasn't so lucky…
Punk…
Faggot…
Bitch…
Punk…
Faggot…
Bitch…

Can't make it go away.
I see black bandanas.
I see figures running out
Of the dark, and I hear
The words.
Loud and sharp.
Punk…
Faggot…
Bitch…
Punk…
Faggot…
Bitch…

TROUBLE

I knew you were going to be trouble
From the moment I locked eyes on you
From across the bar. Tus miradas que
Matan and grin sexy enough to soak my
Chones with precum from just one lick
Of those full lips.

I saw your fresh battle scars from a mile
Away, and damn if they didn't fuel the fire
Beneath me as I slowly realized how
Psychotic you truly were. I never wanted
Any man more than I wanted you when you
Pressed your hardening dick against my leg.

We could have something passionate and
Amazing together. I'm just dysfunctional
Enough to eat your stories right out of the
Hand locked onto my pelos as you
Shoved my head down in between your legs
To taste the sweetest fucking ass I've ever
Tasted, leaving me convinced that
The crazy ones just taste sweeter.

We would be a powerhouse of emotion and
Xicano fucking trying to find truth and safety
And father in long embraces and hours of you
Sitting on my face, hand firmly wrapped around
My cock slowly tracing circles around my foreskin
With beads of precum.

I was smart enough to see right through your
Bullshit. To pretend to be completely
Unfazed by you secretly hiding the fact that you
Are just deep enough under my skin to fuck me
Up royally, knowing damn well I would
Give my left nut to spend the rest of my life
Inside that tight ass of yours.

You see me as a challenge, unlike any man
You've ever met. You pretend to be a hard
Ass who no longer feels anything. But I almost
Drive you crazy melting your walls away
With my fast tongue, warm hands and attention
To detail.

It kills you to find yourself squeezing my
Hand in post coital bliss, our bodies tangled
Together as I sing your favorite song into the
Darkness of the night. We inhale each other and
Nicotine into our lungs slowly killing ourselves with
Addictions to things that are just too bad for us.

You hate how small I make you feel in my arms,
How you find yourself surrendering to my big arms
When I steal a taste of your neck in the dimly lit staircase
As you turn to kiss yourself off my lips
Before you send me back into the night
With hopes of another taste.

You freak at how well I've already memorized your
Body, how I know to breath words on your skin in
Just the right places and how I've learned to be this
Passionate in only 25 years knowing to kiss you on
The nose, and on the inside of your wrists and the
Soles of your feet.

Passion that burns this brightly could only be bad.
I can see us destroying each other at a rapid rate,
Enjoying it in a fucked up twisted act of self-
Destruction worse than Bobby & Whitney,
Britney & K-Fed, Pam & Tommy, Pam & Kid Rock,
AND Amy Winehouse and her needles combined!

I can tell how many tears I will let
Fall at your feet, 13, 527. I know how many cell
Phones I'll break against the wall during our
Arguments, 6. AT&T will cancel my insurance
Because of you. The cops will be called on us
By the neighbors 4 times because of our
Yelling. You will pick a fight with my ex because
Of dirty miradas at the club 9 times. We will
Break 11 glasses, 2 bottles and 1 windshield.
And you know what; the makeup sex would
Make it almost worth it, cabrón!

YOU NEVER CHANGE

You taste bitter and sweet.
You taste that way because you are poisonous.
Poison will kill you
Or at least make you throw up.
That is what this poem is.
It is my purging of thoughts and of your negative energy.

Poison will do something wicked.
It makes you vomit like after hours of crying hysterically
When you broke my heart for what I swore was the last time.
Or after drinking too much alcohol straight from the bottle,
Trying my best to believe you no longer exist.

Bringing you back into my life would be like poisoning
My tired nights with belligerent *"I've always loved you,"*
Text messages. And, *"Can I come over?"* drunk dials.
I can't take you back because weak people
Don't change like they do in the movies.
My head hurts from constantly beating it against a wall.
Closing my eyes as you kiss my erogenous zones won't
Blind me from the reality that you will always go back to
Him when you are sober and hung over in the morning.

I am lonely at night with no one in my bed.
Asking you to come over to cuddle would
Bring me back to falsely loving you with a body
That needs to find meaning again.
I could call every time I'm reminded of an inside joke
We shared. But that would put me back in a rut where
Things repeat themselves. And we repeat ourselves
And fight more than we kiss.

Facing your demons is important.
But what's the point of facing your demons if you
Turn around and sleep with them every night?

Why would I continue to hurt myself over you?
You won't ever love me.
You will only use me for sexual gratification
That will lead to further complication
When your boyfriend catches me in a bad mood
And I corner him and explain to him how you
Suck dick better than any man I've ever met.
Yeah, I know two wrongs don't make a right,
But sometimes slashing his tires makes you feel better.

I can let you sweet talk your way back in with
Thoughts of how things should have been, but slowly
The phone calls stop and I have to relive the way it
Really was, no matter how much it hurt. And you will
Be nowhere to be found even though you promised
Not to leave again.

I could surrender and let you seduce me into your
Bedroom once more, but I know that he is going
To eventually come back to town from vacation wanting his
Boyfriend back. You'll somehow miraculously
Lose my phone number and I won't hear from you again,
Until you're ready to get a lovin' you obviously ain't
Getting from him.

I promise you, I'm not as dumb as you think I am.
What you fail to realize is that I am a vessel of
Light and creation that is sent to spread the

Word of a revolution that doesn't include scared-ass,
Motherfuckin' punk ass bitches like you, who love
To make excuses for simply not knowing what they want
From the world, and take up too much God damned space
Adding nothing new or positive to the world and stealing
Oxygen from the rest of us who could really use it.

One of these days you'll wake up and learn that you
Missed out on something good. You'll find yourself
Remembering the sweet words I spoke,
The way my jaw pops out of place
And that I don't have a gag reflex.
As your head falls back and you moan in ecstasy,
I'll simply slip you a bit of your own poison
And laugh as you scream in pain and
You won't get any help from me and you'll
Wonder why I don't call back...

But you ain't the only one who can lose a
Phone number, bitch.

DÍA DE LOS MUERTOS

For Emanuel Xavier

To you, I offer love and peace.
I offer miles of the finest silk to cover
Your tired body, to keep you
Shimmering with the softest pink, and
Glittery gold and the deepest purple.

I give you food, shelter and fresh
Water when hurricane Katrina ripped
You from the only world you knew
And racism and classism prevented
You from receiving what you needed
To survive.

I give you precious stones, silver earrings,
Cha-cha pumps, come-fuck-me red lipstick,
And a mirror to keep you looking flawless
For all eternity.

I give you glow sticks, false rainbow colored
Eye lashes. A bottle of chilled wine to
Keep the party rolling through the afterlife.

I release light and love
Into the Universe and hope your
Transition is peaceful, beautiful
And magical, just like your spirit was
Here on earth.

This offering is for those who died peacefully
And for those who died in vain.
For those remembered by all and for those
Who died alone, locked away from the world.

For women who rouge their cheeks and curl
Their hair for men who will never love them.
For survivors of rape who died inside
At the first touch of an unwanted hand,
In places still too underdeveloped to feel
Anything but pain and discomfort.
For young girls and boys left struggling to
Reclaim their bodies after having them taken
Too soon by Daddy or tío or big brother.

To those who never found weapons of mass destruction.
For the mothers who will never see their babies again.
For the bodies seen falling from the sky and found under
Mangled metal, glass, soot and ash. For those
Seen floating lifelessly through murky waters filled
With sewage and oil.

This is for God-fearing women who lie and
Cover up bruises to be able to put
Food on their children's table.
For those left for dead or bleeding from
Their stomachs in dark alleys after tricking with
The wrong John.
For those who were caught at the wrong
Place at the wrong time.

For boys who got their asses kicked for walking
With a feminine sway in their hips and
Who couldn't run fast enough to get away.
For those whose cheeks have been struck
By the hands of men who will never see
Their soul through those Papi Chulo eyes.

For those who were hung to sway in the breeze
Because of the color of their skin.

For 12 year old girls who will never understand
The market value of virgin white skin.
For those who felt a world of pain and took a razor
To their own wrists. For those who can't go back to a
Home that no longer exists.

For you, I pray and celebrate your eternal light.

II. UNTITLED CHILDHOOD

OH, FATHER

What would life be like
For me if you stayed
To be a father to your
Only son?

Would you have taught
Me how to be a man?
Would you have taught
Me how to throw and catch
So the jokes wouldn't
Fly all those years in gym
Class? Would you have taught
Me to change my own flat
Tire, so I wouldn't get
Disapproving looks from the
Men that roadside assistance
Sends to rescue me?

Would you have learned
To keep your hands to yourself
And drink less?
Would you ever understand
Why I begged you to buy
Me that yard sale My Little Pony?

Would you be proud of my
Career and read my poetry?
Or would you eventually leave
Anyway because of my love of men?

What would life be like if
You stayed to hug me
Every morning and tuck me
Into bed every night?

Would I still be looking
For you in gay bars
Or under the covers of older
Men's beds, trying to
Find some comfort in strong
Manly arms that aren't yours?

Would I still love the smell of
Cool Water on hairy chests,
Only looking like yours but
Providing a warm place to rest
Long after you left?

If you hadn't disappeared into
The night while I slept,
Would I still grow up to fear
Being abandoned by people I love?

Would I still panic when men take
Longer than normal to call?
Would I rush through relationships
Too quickly because I am afraid
The person will leave at
Any moment, leaving me alone
Again to pick up the pieces
Of a broken home?

Had you stayed and learned
To be a good father and husband,
Would mom still have found
A reason to resent my
Face for looking too much
Like yours? Would I still
Be searching for a mirror
I can't see you in?
Would I still be praying that
you would fade from
My eyes so I no longer
See you staring back at me?

If you stuck it out,
How would you have
Reacted the night I
Confessed to mom I
Was gay? Would you
Disown me also or would
You love me and
Turn away to ignore
It the way you ignored all
The perverse and painful
Things your brothers do to
Their children and wives?

Were we better off without
You? Would I have turned
Out more fucked up being
Raised by you, rather than being
Left with this curse to undo,

Learning to love men who
Look just like you?
Would I still have learned
To hate potatoes if you
Didn't leave us without
Money and nothing else
To eat?

Would I still hate
The smell of bacon if you
Hadn't spent all of those
Years fighting with my mom
As she cooked breakfast?

Would I have still grown to
Hate women named Connie
Or women who so much as
Resembled your mistress?

Would I ever be able to
Shake the pictures from the hallways
Of my mind? Would I still see
Mama there bruised and swollen,
Naked in your arms the
Morning after, when you apologized
And then used her again?

Would I still climb back
Into the closet for mom's
Sake had she not gone
Through all of this and
Survived your marriage to

Keep me alive? Would I
Still owe her so much?
Had you stayed, would I still
Be alive and free?

Would I be dead or locked up
For murdering you the night
You finally succeeded in
Killing my mother?

UNTITLED CHILDHOOD

We were all of 8 years old
When our lips touched for the first time.
He was the first boy I ever kissed.
We were supposed to be innocent children,
But we played house in a special way
We could only have learned from our parents.

I loved when he stayed over at our house,
Because it meant my parents would
Take a break from fighting only long
Enough to keep our family secret from
Leaking out. Watching the way we
Would play together would reveal
That we knew exactly what was going on.

I was the mama, he was the papa.
We would have dinner on a tea set
My father wished his son didn't own.
My memory of his face has faded
With time but I remember that I would
Wait for a look he got in his eyes
Before he would lift his small hand
To slap me across the face.

He would never slap me hard.
We were masters of stage combat
Well before I became a theatre student.
"You fucking bitch!" he would yell, as he
Pulled me up from the floor
That was our dinner table.

"No, please don't!" I would scream as
He pushed me against my closet door
Pretending to choke me.
"I can make you something else for
Dinner. Please don't hurt me!" I would beg.

It was at this moment when he would
Kiss me, still holding his hands to my neck.
He would slap me again as he threw me
Onto my bed covered in New Kids on the Block
Bed sheets and we would kiss again.

With our little hands we would
Reach into each others shorts to rub and grind
Into places that were too underdeveloped to feel.
This was the game we both expected to play
Each time we spent the weekend together.
It became a routine, like watching Saturday
Morning cartoons and something
I missed when it was all over.

Later, after my mom had called game over
Herself, she told me she had gotten word
That he was in an accident that dramatically
Scarred his right leg. He fell out of a moving
Car in the drive thru of a McDonald's and
Was dragged a couple of feet on his side.

I grew instantly sad. I guess I was always
A creature of habit and he was my routine.
He was my cousin.

He was the first boy I had ever kissed.
We were supposed to be innocent children
But we played out in a special way
We could have only learned from our parents.

ALL IN THE FAMILY

At the base of the loma that stretches up
To Memorial High School sits a two-story
Blue and white house. Grandma has been
Gone for years now and the house sits
Filled with memories, occupied by
Tía Nancy, la nasarita, who never married
Because she always has to have things her
Way and no man was going to ever
Change that. Human, spiritual and flawed,
Wrapped up in feminine clothing and sealed in
A thin layer of Rave hairspray. The only
Tía who would give the nieces and nephews
Anything they wanted, spoiling them
Rotten because she had no children of her own.

Tradition runs deep in my family. My house
Is filled with furniture passed down from
Generation to generation, from one house
To the next, and you best not give this shit
Away to someone outside of the family
Or to someone the family has since stopped
Talking to over some random fight or the other,
Because you'll get some rowdy looks from
The Tías who sit around grandma's mesa in the
Kitchen, eating too much and gossiping
Like good Southern Christian women do.

It all stays in the family, like silence, like
Bad habits, like diabetes, like cancer, like
Ignorance, like homophobia, like forced
Christianity, like attitude, like bad tempers,

Like ignoring the bad with fake happiness,
Like alcoholism, like pill popping, like self
Diagnosis, like thinking that all men can be
Good men after a little molding and "he'll
Stop cheating on you or hitting you if you
Pray hard enough."

Grandpa cheated on Grandma the way
My dad cheated on my mom and the way
Many men have cheated on me. There
Has to be a way to honor family tradition
Without remaining stuck in the cycle
Of abuse you were born into before you
Knew how to fear a strong fist or a loud voice.

I'll gladly accept the oak coffee table that was
Passed down to me de la casa de 'uelita,
I'll even take the old upright piano that
Used to annoy mama when I was little.
I want my madrina's collection of music
Boxes, y también quiero la mesa de mi Tía Nancy,
Para poder continuar la tradición de puro
Pinche chisme. But I'll break the cycle of abuse.

I'll remember the man who touched Madrina
Inappropriately. I'll remember how it proved
Too much for her fragile state. I'll remember
That strong foundations still crack. I'll remember
That back in that time, a woman strong
Enough to show weakness could very easily be
Considered insane. I'll remember that she was
Was locked away and strapped to a bed until

She could prove she was no longer unstable.
I'll remember how father pinned mama to the bed.
I'll remember how he'd whip her face with his
Belt until he could see in her eyes that he had
His control again. I'll remember what she looked
Like when it was over, a deflated shell of the
Vibrant woman I knew was my mamita.

I'll remember Joe. I'll remember the moment
I realized that like my mother, I knew how
To react to the look of rage in the eyes of the
Man who promised me the world. I'll remember
The way his voice sounded when
He yelled for hours. I'll feel his weight pressed
Against my body as he tried to get inside.
I'll remember the way his face looked
Through the tears. I'll remember that
Love does exist without power and control.

I'll remember that after all these years, at the
Base of the loma that stretches up to Memorial
High School, sits a two-story blue and white house.
The paint is chipping, and the foundation is cracked,
But this is the place where strong mujeres come
To worship, to nurture, to feed, to heal and
You can always come back here if you need a
Reminder of how strong the roots of your
Family tree truly are.

DADDY

Daddy taught Mama how to love
Again on Culebra Rd and 36th St.
At the car-wash where he worked
Between Fred's Fish Fry with their
Square fish and white bread, and the
Dairy Queen with their chocolate
Dipped cones.

Mama only asked for change to wash
Her car, but the moment she saw
Into his green eyes for the first time,
She was changed forever.

Mama had nothing to lose so it was
No surprise that one week after meeting
Him, she offered to marry him so he
Could get a green card and a shot at
A different life.

She was to marry him on the front
Steps of the courthouse on Valentine's
Day. He'd be free to live his young
Life in anyway he wanted but, her act
Of kindness towards another lost soul
Didn't make sense to him. Along the
Way he fell in love with her and 19
Years later they still sit together on the
Couch late at night watching telenovelas
And eating popcorn.

He was a fighter, a survivor and a damn hard
Worker. From the mean streets of D.F.
To now being the father of two and the
Husband of a wounded woman with a
Whole lot of baggage, he had little time to
Wonder if he had bitten off more than
He could chew. He just went to work.

Daddy didn't speak English. He just
Lowered his head in silence. Daddy
Matched the description of a wanted
Man. Daddy had three blocks to walk
Home from where the workers dropped
Him off at the HEB Mercado on 24th St.
Daddy didn't understand the cops
When they asked him for proper
Identification. Daddy only found three
English words, "Fuck You Motherfucker."

Daddy didn't come home that day and
I saw Mama's heart break again.
She waited by the window in the
Living room, occasionally pulling back
The sheer curtain liner to see if she'd
See him walking down the street
With his lunch box.

I saw a question mark in Mama's
Eyes. She tried to figure out if she
Should be scared for his life, or for
Hers if this meant she had fallen
For another man who only meant to
Hurt her.

No one slept well that night and right
After the sun came up, the phone
Rang. We crowded around the
Phone to hear Daddy's voice. It was
Distant, like it were coming from a another
Part of the world.

Daddy's voice came from the Caseta
In downtown Piedras Negras. They
Sent him back. He hadn't been in the
Country long enough. He didn't have
Proper paperwork to get back into the
Country even with his wife. Luckily he
Had a cousin who lived there who gave
Him a safe place to stay.

Mama was strong. She piled us into
The old Cutlass Supreme that was in
No condition to be making long trips
Into a different country, but with a full
Tank of gas and a Mama full of grace
We made it to Mexico on a prayer,
A bag of Fritos and countless iced cold
Big Reds and Diet 7UPs.

With no idea of how to really get there,
Mama sped her way down to the Tejas
Border and we were in the center of town
Hugging Daddy in no time.

We spent the day in town, and eventually
Found our way to the train tracks

Where coyotes bartered for freedom
In the midday sun. They were asking
For too much money and no guarantee
That Daddy would even get across safely.

There was only one way to make this
Happen. Daddy would swim. He would
Use all of his strength to get across
The Río Bravo to be back in San Antonio
In time for bedtime. He knew he wouldn't
Spend another night without Mama
So his determination pushed him into
The freezing water.

We watched him strip down to the black
Bikini underwear Mama would buy him
At Wal-Mart. He placed all of his clothes
And his shoes into the Plastic HEB bag
That once held our day's ration of food.
He jumped in and we watched him swim
Halfway before we needed to head
Across to meet him in Tejas.

With my feet firmly planted beneath me
In native soul, I watched Daddy risk his
Life to better ours. He made a commitment
That he wasn't backing out of, so he swam.
He fought the current; he fought the cold,
He fought for us and he fought for mama.
The sun was almost out of sight as we
Drove around the foreign streets of
Eagle Pass praying and searching for

A sign, hoping to find Daddy, wet but
Not hurt. We tried hard to avoid Border
Patrol trucks driving around looking for
Daddy or the others who tried to make
It across that day.

We all held our breath every time they
Drove past us. It wasn't easy for us to
Hide in the old Cutlass Supreme because
After all, it was green with bright red
Fenders that didn't match the rest of
The car after it was involved in a wreck.

We circled as the night fell and we saw
No signs of Daddy. Mama slowly broke
Down. I could see fear in her eyes.
I knew this fear far too well.
This was a look I grew up seeing each
Time the bottom would fall out from
Under us and mama would have to
Put the pieces back together.

They say it is the darkest before the dawn,
But dawn came quickly as we turn
The corner to find Daddy walking down a
Street we had driven down 15 times.

He jumped into the backseat and hid.
We all cried. Mama sped away and
Finally got safely onto the highway.

The worst was over, but we weren't
Clear yet. We all knew that halfway
Home from the border was a Border
Patrol Station that would stop us and
Ask Daddy to declare his citizenship.

We practiced with Daddy in the car
Trying to mold his answer into a
Firm "yes," not a shaky "jes." So we
Could finish our journey to the home
He worked so hard to provide for us.
"Are you an American Citizen?" "Jes."
"Jee-es." "Yee-es."

The mile markers flew by and our
Hearts raced in the anticipation of
Driving up to that station. "Yee-es."
"Yes!" There were no lights on. There
Were no state troopers to be seen.
We just sped by in our red and green
Charriot wiping the tears from our eyes.

Daddy was more than a father. He was
A fighter, a survivor and a damn hard
Worker. From the mean streets of D.F.
To now being the father of two and the
Husband of a wounded woman with a
Whole lot of love, he had little time to
Wonder if he had bitten off more than
He could chew. He just got up at 5:00am
The next morning and went to work.

MAMA'S HANDS

I have taken the very worst and the very best from her.
Learning how to be just like her, never straying from the path
She taught me, because I feel like I owe her for keeping me alive.

I don't sleep well because she could only ever hold him off until
Us kids were asleep, and too many times I was shaken from my
Childhood slumber by the sounds of destruction coming from the
Fists of the man who promised her "forever."

I learned how to put her needs before mine, because I will
Never forget walking into their room to see him standing above
Her, whipping her with his belt as she crouched over my little
Brother, shielding him from our father's wrath.

I stress over bills because I remember what it was like to
Eat fried papa tacos every night for dinner for five months
Straight. And even though those bills come every month, on
Time, I am addicted to money and the comfort it brings.

I make myself sick sometimes over the worrying and find
Myself self medicating in a way she taught me how,
Having given me my first anxiety pill when the first day of
Second grade was too much for me to handle.

I have her temper, which only intensifies when we argue
With each other. From her, I inherited my quick wit
And piercing tongue and my ability to know when
Hanging up the phone is the worst thing you could
Do to someone.

I get my compassion from her. Compassion that
Has only grown from moments when I had to be
A caregiver just like her, when it was my turn to
Return the favor.

I have her hands, hands that I studied for hours
As she slept quietly in her hospital bed on the day
The stress, flour tortillas and fried everything
Finally took their toll on her sweet heart.

I will always have that memory with me, the ivy
Piercing, those beautiful hands with perfectly
Manicured nails that she had done the morning
She drove herself to the emergency room.

I will forever be amused by her stubborn nature
That also led her to have her hair done
After having a heart attack, because she knew
She'd have many visitors and wouldn't be seen
With her roots showing.

I get my inability to ask for help from her.
The woman who drove herself to the hospital
Because she didn't want to bother anyone
With her problems, and who always feels
She doesn't need anyone's help.

I get stuck in moments when I am the only person
She shows vulnerability to, like each morning
After my father's cup overflowed and she would explain
Quietly how important it was to never say a word.

After all, the best thing I ever learned from her
Was how to tell a story. How to craft a plotline
As entertaining as anything you'll ever hear.

THE MORE DECEIVED

Ophelia at the banks of Woman Hollering Creek

There's flattery for you,
And repentance.
There's sorrow for you,
And here's some for me.
We may call it your herb of grace on Sundays.

You must wear your sorrow with a difference.
There's your false love.
I'd give you some faithfulness,
But that withered when
My father left.
They say he made a good end.

I now see the most sovereign reason.
Like sweet bells, jangled.
Out of time and harsh.
The unmatched form and stature of blown
Youth, blasted with ecstasy.

O, woe is me to have seen what I have seen,
To see what I see. Why don't you get your
Own mother-fuckin' ass to a nunnery!?
I can't do this anymore.

The sign said 55 miles to San Anto.
As we passed over Woman Hollering Creek,
I let out a yell. Just like Felice in Sandra Cisneros'
Story. I needed to break the silence. I let
Spill forth what I needed to say. Silence sucks.
Sometimes it can't be avoided.

I screamed. We screamed.
Just like the cleaning lady from the bed & breakfast
We just left screamed. She screamed, "Out! Out,
Damned spot! Out, I say!" as she scrubs
The cum-filled sheets from our bed.
The bed where I lay.
Where we lay.
Where you laid me.
Where you laid inside me.
Where I laid inside him,
While you laid inside me.

Hell is murky.
As murky as that chalky substance that
Spilled forth from you time after time.
I did suck the honey from your musicked vows,
Didn't I?

I am angry.
I am angry that you have given me reason
To question my strength.
I'm waiting.
I'm waiting for you to finally gather your
Strength and tell me the truth!

Our relationship was sometimes a paradox.
Now that time gives proof,
You loved me once.
Yes, indeed, my Lord,
You made me believe so.
If that is not the case, if you loved me not,
Then I was the more deceived.

If I was the more deceived,
You are the one who is left with
A stain on the soul.
If you are left with a stain on your soul,
One day you will realize.
When all is said and done,
When you have finally achieved
Revenge on everyone who hurt you,
You will see that you are alone.

Alone with a small pouch of
Remembrances.
Dried up flowers and emotions
That no longer exist.
Remembrances of the one person
Who actually loved you.
Remembrances of the person
You pushed away because
You trusted no one,
Because you were scared.

III. BROKEN SPANISH

HYPNOTIC SOUTHERN COMFORT

The night fell so quickly with the flashing of lights,
Fog rolling into every inch of the bar.
We made moves that night we all thought had been forgotten.
The air had that usual stickiness that most Southern
Nights have; preparing the ground for the coming rain.

"Here's to you, here's to me. May we never disagree.
If we do, fuck you, here's to me!"
One by one, we threw them back like
Salt over our left shoulders to fight off bad luck.
Each of us slowly slipping out of our skins and into each other's,
You felt me, I felt you, you felt just like me.
The insecurities slowly drifting to the top as we learned
To read each other like new books.

Laying together, warm flesh exposed to the cold air.
Goosebumps. Piles of wet clothing scattered throughout
This place we had been so many times before.
It all looking so foreign in this new light.

"I love this song," you whispered into my ear
As I traced my hand across your smooth,
Lean, evenly tanned body. Watching your chest
Rise and fall as I licked the sweet tasting sweat
From the curves on your body.

You learned to surrender to me,
You let me take control the way you liked a man to do.
I honored you. I bowed before you like an altar,
Offering prayers of lust and passion.
The train moved through town, the tracks

So close we could feel the rumble beneath us,
Lending its unmistakable whistle to our ears.
Our bodies moving in motion with it
As the whistle grew closer, so did you.

The lines on your face, every shadow created
By the light above amazed me, touched me in places.
Places that haven't been touched in a long time.
You gently rubbed my back and for once
I was not afraid to respond to your touch.
I just enjoyed the sensual touch of your hands.
For just a few moments, I felt beautiful.
The curves on my body
Were no longer a thing I starved
Myself to get rid of. They were
soft and gorgeous
Like you.

BROKEN SPANISH

I will fuck you in broken Spanish
I will not conjugate verbs correctly
And try to cover it up by performing
Those actions over and over in
Different positions

I will get nervous and sweat, and trip and
Mispronounce words on your skin
As I travel from your neck down to
Your smooth chest, down to your furry
Tummy down to the soles of your feet

I will confuse my tenses and will
Fuck you with no concept of past,
Present or future; taking out aggression
From past lovers, forget who I was
Fucking, and set concrete plans for
Our next encounter

I will overcompensate for my poor
Pronunciation and roll my tongue
With full force as I eat your ass
Leaving my goatee smelling of
Your sweetness for me to enjoy on
The drive home

I will mix up masculine words with
Feminine words, confuse you the top
With me the versatile bottom, flip you
Over and make love to your furry
Ass with no apologies.

I will speak to you in every Spanish
Accent I've ever heard. Go from
"Órale, Chulo, bésame bien fuerte" to
"O sea, ay güey, ¡no mames!" to
*"Coño, carajo. Come on, papi, lemme
See dat cum."* *"¡Zas culera!"*

I will fuck you in broken Spanish
In the only way that I know how
And you will enjoy it like a hot
Pot of fideo from Mama's kitchen
To be eaten with hot, homemade
Cornbread and sliced jalapeños

DIRTY SOUTH

Take me home
Grab me by the hair and
Push me down on my knees
Back down on the
Corner of my old neighborhood
Where cousin Damien,
Who is now in jail, would
Push dime bags of green.

Push me on my back in the
Dry grass and keep me
There with my hands above
My head to surrender
To you and the way you
Make my skin smile.

Let me give myself to your
Full lips and to the ticklish way
Your goatee brushes against
My brown paper bag-colored flesh.
Look into my eyes and
Tell me over and over how good it feels
To be inside…my mind.
Speak to me in the only broken
Spanish you know and beg me
To give you some of this culo.

Whisper words in a nasty way
In the darkness of your eastside hood rich
Bedroom as homegirls walk home
To their moms, staying up late

To comfort their two year old
Children— shaken from
Their sleep by gunshots and
Police car sirens flying by.

Make me your gangsta bitch Barbie doll.
Make me La Sad Gurl to your Ernesto.
Make me want to run to the Flea Market
And airbrush a T-shirt professing my undying
Lust for you.

Give me a full tour of the continent of Africa,
The Bronx, and Mobile, Alabama by tracing
A map on my back with your rough,
Calloused finger tips.
I'll take you on a trip from
Mexico to East L.A.
España all the way back to the west side
Projects of San Anto by drawing a map
On your stomach with my tongue.
Fuck MapQuest.

You've got me so hot I don't
Even care that your butchering my
Language as you grunt the words,
"You want mi leche, Papi?"
Call me Papi because it's the only
Term of endearment you've ever learned.

The way you work your shit does
Enough to make me enjoy the fact
That you are fucking me only because I am Chicano.

I appreciate your Spanish vocabulary
That consists of,
Culo, papi, papa, verga,
Dámelo, chupa, cabrón, oye, loco,
Todo, así, and *coño.*

I appreciate your resourcefulness in
Learning how to structure a sentence
By paying attention to the only Thalía
Song you've heard at the clubs.
I appreciate the commitment and
Energy you put into screaming
"Oye, Papi, ¡dámelo todo!"
Bring me close to the edge with each
Smack of your hand on my ass and
The sheer thought of our
Forbidden equal opportunity, affirmative
Action action.

Make me cum with visual images of brown
Skin on brown skin, thin fingers
Wrapped around thick braids,
Ancient eyes piercing the darkness
And a deep understanding of safety
In each other's arms.

I want to write words of power
On your skin in permanent marker
So they never fade, so we can
Always remember each emotion
As strongly as we feel them now.

Collapse on top of me in a pile of
Sweaty flesh pinning me to your
Bed, promising not to move or pull out
So I can stay here until I die or
Fall asleep in your arms to
Dream of far off places, forbidden
Ideas and the love of my home.
I'm home in your bed where I can enjoy
The warm Southern summer
Night with you.

SIN

Tonight you exist to inspire.
Tonight we wrap ourselves
In bright colors and
Make the art on the
Walls come to life.

Tonight we follow Huitzilopochtli
To el águila y la serpiente.
Where soul meets spirit,
Where celestial father meets
Earth mama and the sun
Sinks deep into the land.

Tonight will be a battle
Of good and evil as
El diablo tries to kill
The angelito with feathered
Wings the color of virgin snow.

Tonight as your lips
Melt into mine and
Piel morena spills
Over piel canela the
Struggle will prove
That I have already
Been conquered, my
Femininity vanquished
To another land.

Tonight we cross borders
And try to build bridges
Over the choppy waters of
Gender roles and a sea of
Preconceived notions.

Tonight we paint each other's
Bodies with sweat as
The rosary dangles from
My neck into your mouth as
I hover above you, your legs
Wrapped around my waist,
Your hips thrusting upwards
Towards heaven.

Tonight we sin, tonight we
Break rules, tonight we release.
Tonight you exist in art form
And become immortalized in ink.

GLOW

He found mystery in my eyes as
He caught a glimpse of my face in the
Dim glow of the movie screen.

I wanted to kneel at his altar.
Worship in his ancient temple;
Chant over and over,
Having memorized every word.

My hand moved south as
I prayed to the God of myself,
Jaguar Mistress in the dim glow
Of an adult film playing in the background.
Trying to lure him in.

Across the dark theatre
Filled with men.
Men.
Men with wives who had no idea.
Above the blow jobs.
Above the hand jobs.
Stale smell of cum
Saliva
Mint
Clorox Bleach
Moaning, slurping
Slurping, slapping
Slapping, stroking
I met his eye again.

He was smooth,
No hair,
Save for the trail.
Bush.
Underarm.
I worshiped his feet.

Then he disappeared.
I could never have him by day,
Our relationship exists only in night.
I am invisible to the sun,
I remain alone until nightfall,
Where this love glows in the dark.

PLAYFUL PAINTER

Tell my story in bright colors and glitter
Speak to me through brush strokes
On my tired back as you make Queer
Aztlán come to life on my bare skin.

Paint my panza with a prettier picture
And cover my lonjas in delicate shades
Of pink and lavender to cover up the
Times when mama showed her love
Through tacos, arroz or weenie con egg.

Trace my foreskin with silver
Make it attractive to all men.
Make it a delicious sight and make their
Tongues crave it's taste the way you
Crave menudo after too much drinking.

Cover my chest in metallic gold
Make me regret passing
Judgment before, as you make me
Crave your hot piss on my body as
You stand above me with that look
In your eyes.

Sing to me from your canvas in a
Language only I could understand
Because I, too, have been called
Insane and because I, too, have
Been misunderstood.

Paint us onto the shores of Papalotlan
Where bright color winged-butterflies
Make love on our naked
Bodies in ways we've been told
Were wrong or perverse.

Rub cold, wet paint into my shoulders
As we sip Champagne from kitchen
Glasses and inhale Jesus' snow covered
Feet to help us reach a higher level
Of consciousness where we'll create
New Xicano folklore that won't
Be washed away by the hardest rainstorm.

SLEEP SOUNDS

Nights in San Antonio have a familiar
Sound. The sound creeps through the
Open bedroom window, falls upon
Us both as we sleep in each other's arms.

The sound mixes naturally with the soft
Buzz of your gentle snore, marking the
End of another busy day. I lose myself
In this symphony, my hand on the
Curve of your hip— my
Favorite part of your body.

Cars whiz in the distance,
Down I-35. Some people rolling into
Work still drunk from the night's festivities.
Some, mujeres on their way
To the taquerías that will fill our panzas with
Breakfast tacos y cafecito later in the day.

Your cuerpo shakes a little bit as a breeze
Blows night air across your chest, this being
One of the last mild nights of Tejas springtime,
The neighbor's dog yelps, trying to
Find a place to pee during his midnight walk,
And that pinche gato that only seems to be in heat
When we crave sleep the most.

You turn and wrap your leg around
Me as the last Amtrak train rolls through the
Eastside, rumbling loudly on the tracks, blowing
A warning whistle that grows louder and
Louder as it picks up speed.

A sprinkling of helicopters whirling, and the
Occasional police siren remind me of my
Childhood. These urban sounds that might be
Disturbing to some, relax me and lull me to sleep.

These sounds remind me of why I returned
Home. They remind me of warm,
Safe places. Like mama's arms when I was
Scared, or Grandma's kitchen when the tías
Sat around laughing from their panzas.

Bedtime was when I fought to stay up and
Watch *Three's Company* on the arm of Tía
Nancy's Lazy Boy, listening to her drift away,
Lulled to sleep by the sounds of Nick at Night.

Now, bedtime is when I explore
Your beautiful body, kneading
The stress away with love. It is the series
Of besitos that I leave across your back
And the goose bumps rising on your flesh.

It is a time of tranquility and silence, save
For the soft moans that circle above us as
We settle into the cold bed sheets that wrap
Us in night time and send us off to slumber
In each other's arms.

These arms, these legs, these sounds, and
We, are one. Juntos en nuestra cama,
Con el sonido de la ciudad, we collide
In the dreams filling my head, my heart
That is filled with you, and my soul that
Is filled with the poetry of your beautiful
Brown skin.

YOU WERE GOING TO BE A GREAT POEM

I began to write the poem
In my head the moment
Our eyes met across
The crowded room.

My mind worked overtime, beginning
To imagine the ways you could
bring my body to ecstasy.

My eyes undressed you, slowly.
Pealing away the layers of your
Gruff exterior. One Fubu item at
A time. Leaving only a pair of Tim's
And a smirk.

Your body rocked side to side to
The beat as I turned on a little
Hip hop charm hoping to catch your eye.

As the disco ball spun above our heads,
I couldn't get you back home soon enough,
Brief goodbyes, a walk to the car, and a quick
Drive home brought us to that dark wooden
Table where we got lost in sweet talk and a
Fat blunt you rolled with your bare hands.

I closed my eyes and braced
Myself for what I imagined would
Be a sinful night of cholo loving,
My hips couldn't stay still as you
Moved onto the bed next to me.

I held my breath and I grasped at
The bedsheets at my side as you
Parted your lips to say something.

You asked for a towel. It had only
Been three minutes and you were
Finished before I could even take my
Clothes off and join the party.

You were going to be a great poem
But I don't write anything shorter than
Three minutes.

OCTAVE OF EASTER

Meet me tomorrow night in the
Garden of Gethsemane. We
Will give Judas a run for his money,
Burning pages of the great book
With the friction of two Xicano men
Moving in that the way Mama said
Would send me straight to hell.

Meet me under the paschal full moon.
End your liturgical season of
Fasting and self denial with passionate
Bites on the side of my neck.
Rip the rosario from my chest
Letting the prayer beads fall onto
The soil at the foot of this Mount of Olives.

Let Califaztlán collide with Tejaztlán,
One thrust at a time, from Easter Day
To Ascension Day. Spending 40 days and
40 nights inside that culo you once
Fingered through dark denim jeans
In the dark smoky room that became
The tomb of all those beliefs
Once shoved down our throats by wooden
Rulers, monjas and mothers with catholic guilt.

Let's run barefoot through fields of
Blue bonnets and Tejas sagebrush.
Accept my offerings of almsgiving,
Smear my back with your sudor
And spit. Whisper prayers

Onto my back, forcing the pelitos on
My neck to stand and rejoice in
Celebration, bearing witness
To our sacrament. I am newly
Baptized in your arms.

Heal the small scar on the small
Of my back, where he once left me
Bleeding and empty. Bring my
Soul back to life as the rubber band
Around your thick ponytail busts,
Your hair a crown of thorns falling
Around my face. Your chest
Pressing against my back,
With my hands pinned to the bed
At my sides.

Suck the mercy from my lips,
Surrender all your convictions.
Let politics fade long enough
For me to flick my tongue
Up and down your indígena skin
As the flickering lights of two lit
Velas on the altar burn for your
Protection and the miracle of
Of feeling a man inside of me again.

Con la mano poderosa guiding
Us gently upwards, you
Softly snore with the bedsheet
Randomly thrown across your

Panza, brazos intertwined with
Mine. In this moment, to see you
In his image, to see the image of
Him in your face, beautiful, brown
Xicano and proud, brought me
Closest to the heaven we try to
Escape everyday.

Santo Niño de Atocha at our feet,
Watching over, freeing us from guilt
And punishing looks. Heaven feels
Just right if it means we can stay this
Way: a mess of cum, sweat, babas y pelo;
Only for a while, if not for forever.

IV. FOOL'S PARADISE

WITHDRAWAL

I watched the sun rise on your stubble.
I watched the sky go from twinkling
Texas twilight to gorgeous autumn
Morning in the last hour I knew I had
To spend in your arms, before
The alarm clock sounded and you
Would be taken from my bed.

I let you hold me through the night
And committed your sleep sounds
To memory as you slowly drifted
Into slumber at my side, your hip
Fitting perfectly like a puzzle piece
Against mine.

You woke me up with a gentle
Kiss, not even having the
Patience to wait until I
Brushed the sleep out of
My mouth. You kept kissing
Until you climbed on top of me
And put your nose to my chest
To breathe me in.

You said my clothes smelled
Of the fabric softener that filled
The air in your grandma's house.
You took comfort in that and I
Caught you smelling me over and
Over when I wasn't looking.

I let you examine my body with
Your strong hands as I rested
My head in the pillow and you
Firmly massaged my back,
Running your fingers down my
Spine and caressing my sensual
Spots with extra care.

In one night you managed to
Replace a world of mixed signals
And unspoken feelings with pure
Desire, taking in every bit of me.
You knew it was what you
Wanted and your lips and teeth
And hands and legs clearly
Communicated that all night.

I like this distraction. I crave you.
I curse the alarm clock that
Rings too loud and takes you from
Me. I want to spend more time
Getting lost in your eyes. I want
To stay under the covers until the
Day turns to night and into day again.

FOOL'S PARADISE

Just for tonight, I want
You to hold me in your
Arms. Don't make me sit
And wonder if you are
Going to call.

Fall asleep with your forehead
Against the nape of my neck
And rock me to sleep with
The sound of your breathing.

Rub my shoulders and listen
To me bitch about my day.
Make me forget about why I
Was bitching with a simple
Kiss on my forehead or one
Twirl of my hair.

Let's forget about the
10 million reasons why
A relationship between
Us will never work.

Right now, I just need you
To lay with your head on
My chest for hours as we
Watch movies on my
Couch instead of going
To the club on Saturday night.

Don't let me go straight
To bed when the lights
Go out. Kiss me over
And over and make me
Feel sexy.

Make me forget that I
Can't fit into my skinny
Jeans right now and just
Love me the whole
Night long.

This situation will never
Be perfect. It will never
Be seamless. But right
Now, just undress and take
Your place on your side of
The bed and we'll forget
We broke up a year and a
Half ago.

We will follow our old
Routine as if no time
Had ever passed. I
Will sleep peacefully
With your hip pressed
Against mine, until
Sunday morning comes
And we can lounge around
The house all day the
Way we always did.

A FUCKING POEM

I want you to fuck a good poem out of me.
Not a poem about animalistic, lust but
Candles lit, soft music playing kind of lovemaking.
The kind I have never been comfortable enough
To experience while sober.

I want you to suck sweet words from my lips.
Words that transcend time and will linger in the
Air when you've already gone home. Words that
Move mountains with their pure intensity and
Leave me weak in the knees from
Shear intoxication.

I want you to lick the insecurity off of my skin.
Insecurity from years of being told fat is ugly
And from guys who treated my body like
Something that wasn't worth worshiping. Chip
Away at my walls with your tongue, getting me
To slowly open up further and further to let you in.

I want you to finger an epic poem out of me.
A poem that will last for hours, not some haiku
That skims the tip of the iceberg and leaves me
Wanting more and more and more. Give me the
Inspiration to fill a book with one experience,
Not a half ass story that has to be
Filled-in with three other experiences to even
Complete one poem.

I want you to kiss away the pain of my past.
A pain that I can't seem to let go of no matter how
Hard I try. A pain that no man has ever tried

To get rid of, or tried to make a little
Easier to handle. Kiss my eyes closed at night
And hold me; but mean it. Don't hold me because
You think you have to, hold me because you
Want me in your arms.

I want you to fuck a good poem out of me.
Make love *and* hate to me and inspire my
Next masterpiece. Move me physically
And figuratively, allowing me to paint you
Pictures of simple beauty.

UNSCRIPTED

A poem written in the corner of
a leather bar during a full moon.

You are that poem I've been trying to
Write for almost four months now, but that
Keeps getting stuck somewhere under stacks
Of academic writing and training manuals.

You are the smile on my face that has been
Missing in action for five years now.
I have trouble looking at myself in the mirror
When we hang up the phone because feel silly.

You are that ticklish feeling I get
When you kiss my forehead over and over.
Those butterflies in my stomach that
I thought migrated south for the winter
And never came back.

You are that nervous feeling I used to get
While passing notes to my grade school
Crush posing questions like, "Do you want
To go around? Circle: Yes or No."

You are silly noises made during cuddle
Sessions and tickle wars that are probably
Too silly to be having as adults.
The total sense of defiance we show as we chase
Each other down aisles of supermarkets,
Laughing with fingers extended ready to tickle.

You are the feeling I have that all love songs
Were written by me for you. The funny
Desire I have to blast those songs as I
Sing full voice while speeding down I-35 trying
To get to you as quickly as I can.

You are the voice that has me saving each
Voicemail you leave. The voice that
Melts my heart as quickly as a slab of
Butter placed on the hot piece of bread
We would get on fieldtrips to the
Buttercrust Bakery.

You are that burning desire to profess true
San Anto emotion during a radio show's
Slow jam dedication hour. Silly songs burnt
To a CD that mean so much because any child
Of the 80s knows that no matter the format,
It's still a mix tape.

You are a kiss on the hand that quickly slaps the
Roof of the car while driving under a yellow light,
And two feet that come off the floorboard while
Driving over train tracks, and a quick wish at
11:11 pm because I'm not doing anything to
Jinx any of this.

You are a guilty pleasure, like *America's Next
Top Model* marathons on Saturday mornings,
Britney Spears songs, peanut butter
Straight from the jar, cold pizza for breakfast,
Or Girl Scout Cookies and chocolate milk.

You are a sudden realization that all of the
Crap I went through in my past helped me
Be a better, stronger, and wiser man that
Can now meet you somewhere in the middle
Of all of this, to be your partner in crime.

CHASING SCARS

I want to hug away your past.
I want to put my big arms around
You and never let go. Just in case
The bullshit tries to come back
And mess things up.

I want to rub away the pain
From the men who hurt you
Con una sana sana colita de
Rana. And stick around just in
Case you don't sana hoy,
You can sana mañana.

I'm bleeding again as I find
Myself picking at my scabs,
Getting closer to someone
New. I keep thinking the
Bottom is going to fall out
And it'll all crumble around
My feet like it always has.

Only I hear sincerity every
Time you speak. I see your
Soul every time you look
Into my eyes. I feel your
Heart every time you trust
Me enough to open up about
Something de los años pasados.

The smell of your cologne
Lingers on my car seats.
Memories of us spending

Time together keep playing
Back in my head like old
Black and white movies.

I keep trying to chase
Away the scars that run
Too deep, so that insecurity
And self hatred don't
Try to take over again the
Way they like to when things
Start to get good.

Instead, I will force myself
To enjoy, not question.
Not rush, just be, and enjoy
A new friend with a new
Outlook. Enjoy my new
Source of inspiration, let
The fresh air fill my lungs,
And dive head first into
The future.

THIN LINE

You rode away on the last bus out of town.
I kept to my bed as the storm blew in.
The rain fell in large drops and lighting turned
Night to day. The thunder was loud, as if it
Were trying to say something.

I stood in my bathroom mirror after trying to
Wash you off of my tired body. I traced my
Fingers over my damaged skin to count each
Bruise and scratch you left behind. The one
On my right shoulder glows an angry red, the
One on my left a dark purple.

My cheeks grew hot as I tried to figure out which
Part of this was to be sexy to me. I followed
The bruises down to my forearm. Only three
Bruises will be hard to hide. And one scratch
Where your teeth broke the skin.

There is a thin line between love and hate.
Between you hurting me so good and you
Making me bleed. Between a little tug of the
Hair, firm slap on the ass or gentle nibble of
My flesh, and the sorry condition you left
My body in.

I turned to examine my back and found the
Series of bite marks you left across my shoulders.
The dark purple marks seemed to form wings
Across my back but you never learned how to
Love an angel. You became mean and uncaring
As you claimed your prize after marking your territory.

My mind wandered again trying to figure out
Just how many men had found the way you fuck
Exciting. I tried to figure out how many of them
Let you ram your fat dick in with no lube.
I tried to find the sweetness in the words, "Loosen
The fuck up."

I had trouble remembering what I did that would
Give you an idea that I would be the one you
Could do this to. Did me nibbling on your ear,
Letting you put your hand up under my shirt
In public or boldly kissing you in the bright
Lighting of an IHOP give you some idea
That I would enjoy being torn
To pieces by your bare teeth?

I was looking for the wrong thing in your lips
And in the way you licked my neck in public.
I tried to find it with the wrong man in my bed
Yet again and now have two scars to remind
Me of what Crown and 7-up can do to some
People.

I was foolish enough to think I could escape
My pain in the only way I had in the past, and
Manage to keep control of the situation this time.
I found a false sense of security in a cold
Bud Light and the coy, shy smile
Of a sexy ass peloncito.

V. CHASING SCARS AWAY

GARDEN OF MY SOUL

You wanted to conquer this body,
Leave me with no resources to
Make a better life for myself.

You wanted me to rely on you,
So you could feel the power you
Thought you had over me.

You left me when I was only 8 years old.
Every time someone else moves on,
Even if not to abandon me, I am that 8
Year old boy all over again.

You wanted to strike the fear of God
In me. A God I no longer pray to
Because for all these years, the prayers
Didn't make the ghosts go away.

You wanted to crush me beneath
Your fist so you could feel like a
Strong man. All you did was
Make me a stronger man than you.

You wanted to beat my mother
In front of me so we'd be too
Scared to say a word, but she
Was always stronger and got out.

You left this young body,
Chubby and naked, yearning
For attention. Scars set deep
Within bruised flesh and you
Never looked back. Not even once.

You wanted me to believe
I could never save myself
From the hell you left me to rot in.
I will be a better father than you.

I will be a better lover, son, brother,
Educator, lifesaver, peacemaker,
Shit starter, breaker of silence,
Thought provoker, love maker,
Hip shaker and tradition breaker,
Than you ever had the creativity
To imagine for yourself to be.

When the cold rain falls, I
Will have the sense to not run
From it. I will let it wash over me,
And stand strong, knowing you
Did not win this war.

Where you left this land,
Raped and ravaged, you left
A place where new seeds
Will be planted and nurtured by
A family of my choosing. Beautiful
Brown jardineros with green
Thumbs who know how to make
The garden of my soul grow.

BAKERMAN

You were happy to see me.
I pretended not to see you.
You waved,
I forced a smile.
I tried to be excited.
I can't pretend you didn't ruin my life.
I'm happy you got fat.

TO THE MAN WHO WILL CAUSE
MORE HARM THAN GOOD

You are damn cute, pa.
From your coarse head
Of hair to the bottom
Of your feet that brought
You from the island of
Puerto Rico to Texas,
With all but $20 in your pocket.

You ain't the first and
Probably not the last
Man who tried to step
To me when his boyfriend
Wasn't looking. Mama didn't
Raise no fool.

You drive me crazy, pa.
Your thick accent and
The bass in your voice.
Your swagger, your
Smooth talkin' ass
Turn me out with
A quickness.

Shit is complicated and
Although multiple realities
Exist in the world at the same
Time, I want to be someone's
Primary love and not end
Every night with - *that*
Won't happen again until
I'm single.

I want you some more, pa.
I want to feel your moderately
Hairy body pushing against my
Back. The smell of beer breath
Filling the air around us
As your ear fetish explores
My lobes from behind.

You are too afraid of what
Life would be like without
Him and I can't afford this
Karma. Looks like you not only
Have good dick, daddy. But
You also got a world of drama
That follows, and I only deal
With that shit on stage, mic in
Hand, all lights on me.

Fix your shit, pa.
So we can rock the bed
Again without time limits.
So you can stay a little
Longer without having to wash
Me off your skin with the
Fear that he's gonna smell
My breath on your cock.

WHILE MY PEN GENTLY WEEPS

You walked away with all of
My options in your pocket on
a cold winter's night. The
stars dimmed in the bright
light of a waxing moon
while my pen gently wept.

I can't bring myself to admit
That you were right and I was wrong.
That we were not good for each other.
This isn't pride. This is pain.
Burning like Daddy's Salsa.

You are now just some poem that
I once wrote and about four others
That I could never finish. Maybe
On another day I will be able to
Finish these love poems with happier
Endings, but still my pen gently weeps.

I almost wish that you were the
Lying kind of guy so I wouldn't
Be left alone with the truth of
You in the arms of someone else
And the realization that I no longer
Have the freedom of saying, "I love
You, cabrón."

You are now just a song that
Once stuck in my head like chicle.
The song I would sing at the top of

My lungs in the shower or in the
Car while stuck in rush hour traffic.
Soon I won't even remember
The words. Still my pen gently weeps.

I will lose myself in one too many
Drinks and try to keep myself
From dialing your number late
At night for any bit of comfort
That you used to provide. Even
Though I can still feel your lips
On the small of my back.

You are now just a dance that
I won't offer to any other man,
Knowing that I will never feel this
Way in the arms of anyone else.
I will just sit with the tías
At the table eating peanuts and
After dinner mints at family
Weddings and Quinceañeras,
Until someone else comes along
To teach me a different dance.

I will slice open my venas and
Let these words spill out onto
Paper as you hold my heart in
Your hands that exist to love
Someone else one soft caress
At a time.

You are now just a dream that
Reoccurs night after night and
That always ends the same
Way. One day I will hopefully
Be able to dream another dream
That will allow me to rise with
Dry eyes, but for now my pen
Gently weeps.

I will try to fill the
Spaces, wash the smell of you
Out of my hair, shake the image
Of you from my mente, train
My heart not to miss you late
At night when my pen gently weeps.

REALIZATION

Straight men used to be my specialty.
But I decided to trade them in for
Emotionally unavailable gay men who
Don't know what they want.

Then I stopped dating altogether.
I grew sick of all of the games.
I went seven months without
Cleaning my house.
It wasn't until I realized my birthday
Was quickly approaching and I still
Had my cake from the year before,
Growing moldy in the fridge, that I
Snapped out of it.

Now I am getting better, I can
Only fall so far before all I can go is up.
My moment of awakening
Wasn't really dramatic. It wasn't as
If all of sudden things were clear
As crystal. It wasn't like things were
Clear enough to see all the way into
Tomorrow. It was just like changing an old
Light bulb. The overhead lighting was now
Too bright and revealed a thick layer of
Dust all over everything.

I realized too much all at once.
I realized you were never
Going to settle down with me.
So I could stop dreaming of the life

I wanted us to share.
I realized that no matter how
Badly I tried, I would never
Look like the boys you run after.
So I should move on and be happy
For you and your new boyfriend.

I realized that sleeping with guys
Every time you made me mad
Didn't even the score or make
You jealous. It just made me lonelier.

I realized there was no way you
Would leave your boyfriend for
Me. Sleeping with you behind his
Back didn't mean you were going
To fall in love with me.
It just made me stuck in a place
I didn't want to be.

I realized that I could eat an
Entire pack of Double Stuf Oreos
At one time, but that wasn't
Going to provide comfort.
It just made me fat and addicted
To processed sugar.

I realized that I spent $100 a
Week on alcohol but I didn't find
Answers at the bottom of an Absolut
Citron bottle. It just made me

A drunk ass bitch.
I realized that going on a shopping
Spree every time you made me
Feel worthless wasn't going to fulfill
Any part of me. It would only make me
A broke-ass bitch.

I realized that crying myself to sleep
Over the men I missed didn't
Make me a bad feminist.
It just made me human.

I realized that recycling sleepless
Nights and swollen eyes and splitting
Headaches into art didn't make me
Over-dramatic. It just made me a poet.

HOLLOW

I am only the shell of the man
My parents wish I were
So it's a complete surprise
That I bleed as much as I do
When you cut me.

I am hollow. So when you
Place me to your ear you can
Actually hear the sounds of
My broken past.

Sounds of breaking glass, holes
Being kicked into walls, and
Deep voices shouting into the
Night are amplified by father's rage.

If you listen carefully, you can
Hear the softest of sounds. Like the
Needle slowly stitching up Mama's
Forehead right at her color treated
Hairline, where Father broke open
A 40 oz beer bottle.

You can place your ear to my
Chest and hear Mama's soft voice
As she teaches us the made up
Story to explain to guests how
The holes got into the wall.

You can hear seagulls and the waves
Of the Gulf of Mexico crashing onto

The Texas coast, just down the sandy
Hill from our condo where we
Played perfect family.

You can hear the sound of a bowl
Crashing into the sink, and Mama's
Voice screaming about how she
Sacrificed everything and risked
Her life too many times to have
Her son not get into heaven for
Being gay.

You can hear Tías' voices ask if
I ever plan on finding a woman
To marry. And in the same breath
Ask if I have any suggestions
For window treatments to match
The new couch.

You can hear the sound of a fist
Hitting bare skin. And the loud voice
Of the first man who ever hit me,
Right before he tried to rob me of
An innocence that had been long gone.

You can hear my tears falling into
Puddles around my feet. And the voice
Of the first man who cheated on me
And was dumb enough to get caught,
Trying to convince me to remain his friend.

You can hear young male voices
Shouting profanities, because their
Mamas never taught them no better,
As they surround me and make
Me their victim.

Making me a victim yet again.
I scramble to heal, trying hard to
Survive this and not be another
Statistic, having made one dumb
Decision that almost cost me my life.

You can hear Mama's voice again
Spouting off some bullshit she
Learned from watching Oprah.
You can hear the faint cry
From my wounded heart,
Just begging for a hug as I try to
Convince myself that I didn't
Deserve this.

You can hear Tío's accordion playing
Over the crackling fire as we sing
Drunken Rancheras into the full moon.
And my boyish giggle as he moves his
Hands up under my shirt in the way I'm
Sure he wished my Tía would let him.

You can hear my silent prayers
Of shame, asking for forgiveness
On the night I learned how to

Masturbate to the thoughts of Tío's
Mustache on my chest when he
Would kiss my nipples.

You can hear Selena's voice and
Botines stomping a cumbia on the
Dance floor of the Silver Dollar,
Filled with men who turn me on
For looking just like Tío— all dirty
In their own special way.

You can hear cum splattering
Onto the walls of my stomach
As I swallowed the "love" of the
First straight man I ever scored.
And the sounds of wasted, sacred
Life coating my rectum because,
If he wanted to use a condom, he'd
Sleep with his girlfriend.

I do not bleed for being full of life.
I simply spill forth the blood
Of my memories that lurk inside of
Me, begging to be heard from
The pit of my stomach through my
Hollow frame.

Their sounds echo so loudly
That sometimes I can't think
Straight. I reach through them
And try to pull out art, but even

That doesn't work sometimes.
On quiet, lonely nights like this
You hear the noises, all milling
Around and bouncing off of my
Heart. You hear them banging
Against my lungs, leaving them
Sore like a cigarette hangover.

The sounds are sometimes so
Crippling that they bring me to
My knees in prayer, hoping to
God that I'm not crazy, and that
They will eventually fade away,
Making room for real life to grow.

DOS POETAS LOCOS

I was saving this poem for you.
I hid it away, deep down where
No one would find it. I wanted to
Wait until I could whisper it to you
In the darkness of a small smoky
Bar, thighs pressed together as we
Told stories to the soundtrack of
A San Antonio jukebox.

I was saving this poem for you.
I hid it in the rhythm of my hips
That moved across a crowded
Dance floor, with the pride of
Knowing a cute jotito just
Formally asked me to dance
With him the moment the
Selena Megamix started to play.

I was saving this poem for you.
I hid it in my distinctive laugh,
And let it wash over you night
After night as we exchanged
Secrets. Spilling juicy details
Across the table like the cold
Cerveza, spilling from the half
Empty bottles in our hands.

I was saving this poem for you.
I hid it in the pit of my stomach
Where the laughter lives.

The place we feed at 3 am, chisme
Con queso, breakfast
Tacos con salsa, menudo y
Barbacoa, aguacate y horchata.

I was saving this poem for you.
I hid it in a corner of my mind,
And let you catch a glimpse of it
Every time you went for a run
Through the crazy place my
Brain calls home. It was there
entre memorias I'm sure you could swear
Were yours, as we were cut
From the same mold.

I was saving this poem for you.
I hid it in my brown eyes that
Could only look at you with
Admiration and longing,. A longing
Deeper than any man could express.
Knowing that this love is about
Familia and about creativity and
About knowing each other in ways our partners,
Lovers, tricks, mistakes, ex's, or tricks–
Turned–lovers–turned–partners–turned
Mistakes, could never know us.

I was saving this poem for you.
I hid it in my hands, hands that don't
Understand that you have issues being touched.

Hands that want to hold the small of your
Back when we walk in public, regardless
Of who is around. The hands that want to
Touch your face upon the delivery
Of every funny story.

I was saving this poem for you.
I hid it just under my skin, a similar
Shade to yours. Skin covered in a dusting
Of salt and pepper hair, skin that is prone
To sweating when a cute boy walks in the
Room or simply from the oppressive south
Texas sun. The sweat still spilled from our
Pores and we spent long days not caring
That it coated our sticky skin and loved
Each other completely.

I was saving this poem for you.
I hid it in my entire being and lived it
Before I could capture it on paper to
Give to you as a gift of thanks. A thank
You for the uncontrollable laughter,
The tears, the history, the food, the
Drink, the movement, the sweat, and the
Arte that we let our souls create
In a time where many find it hard
To catch a single glimpse of light.

I was saving this poem for you.
Now, it is yours forever.

DINO FOXX, born and raised in San Antonio, Texas, is a nationally

presented actor, singer, dancer, writer, spoken word poet, hip-hop artist, arts educator and activist. He is a founding member of Tragic Bitches (a Queer Xicana/o Performance Poetry Collaborative), a company member with Jump-Start Performance Co. and an emcee with the band, The Push Pens. Andrés Duque of Blabbeando has described his poetry as following "themes of family unity and disunity, ethnic bonds and divisions, assimilation and displacement as well as sexuality and love." His poetry has been published in such collections as *Mariposas: A Modern Anthology of Queer Latino Poetry* (Floricanto Press), the 19th issue of *Suspect Thoughts: A Journal of Subversive Writing* (2007) and *Queer Codex: Chile Love* (Evelyn Street Press/allgo). Foxx will also be featured in the upcoming poetry collection *Joto: An Anthology of Queer Xicano & Chicano Poetry* through Kórima Press.

As a member of the artistic company at Jump-Start, Dino Foxx has produced, written for, worked on the technical team of, or performed in over 50 original performances including *Epcot el Alamall* developed with Guillermo Gomez-Peña (2004), *Memoirs of a Jot@ - Part 1* (2007), and *Last Call for Truth* written with Manuel Cros Esquivel and Billy Muñoz.

As his fire-eating gender-bending burlesque alter-ego Foxxy Blue Orchid, Foxx produces and performs as a member of the Stars and Garters Burlesque All-Star Cast and is a co-producer and host for the San Antonio Burlesque Festival.

OTHER KÓRIMA PRESS TITLES

Amorcito Maricón
        by Lorenzo Herrera y Lozano

Brazos, Carry Me
        by Pablo Miguel Martínez

Ditch Water
        by Joseph Delgado

Empanada: A Lesbiana Story en Probaditas
        by Anel I. Flores

Las Hociconas: Three Locas with Big Mouths and Even Bigger Brains
        by Adelina Anthony

Joto: An Anthology of Queer Xicano & Chicano Poetry
        edited by Lorenzo Herrera y Lozano

Tragic Bitches: An Experiment in Queer Xicana & Xicano Performance Poetry
        by Adelina Anthony, Dino Foxx, and Lorenzo Herrera y Lozano

Made in the USA
San Bernardino, CA
22 March 2014